Oh No! Fred Wet the Bed

Written by Craig Biss

Illustrated by Anne Celesta Stevens

To every kid who has ever woken up to a wet bed and wondered what is wrong with them. If you have ever been bullied because of this... Nothing is wrong with you!

Your body is growing, learning, and figuring things out one night at a time. Some lessons just take a little longer, and that is okay. You are not alone, you are not broken, and you are definitely not the only one this has happened to.

There are millions of kids, and even grown-ups, who once stood right where you are now. One day, sooner than you think, this will simply be something you used to do when you were little.

Until then, remember this:
You are brave.
You are strong.
You are learning.
And a wet bed can never change how special you are.

This book was written for you!

With encouragement and a big high-five,

Craig Biss

Oh No! Fred Wet the Bed

Copyright © 2019 by Craig Biss

Illustrations © 2019 Anne Celesta Stevens.

ISBN-13: 978-1-949439-05-2

Disclaimer

This book is intended for educational and entertainment purposes only. The information and suggestions presented in this story are not intended to replace professional medical advice, diagnosis, or treatment.

Bedwetting can have many causes, and every child is different. Parents or caregivers who have concerns about a child's health or development should consult a qualified healthcare professional.

The author and publisher are not responsible for any actions taken based on the content of this book.

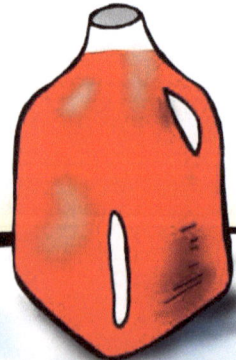

Presented to:

_____

From:

_____

Date:

_____

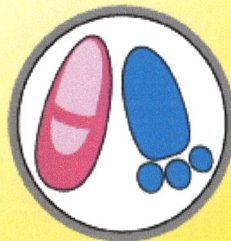

There once was a kid named Fred and every night, he wet the bed. His sheets went splash and pillow said, "Whoa there, Fred... not again, Fred!"

"Oopsy!"

One day after school, Fred spoke to his best friend, Ted. Ted knew an older kid named Ned, who promised he could help Fred quit wetting the bed.

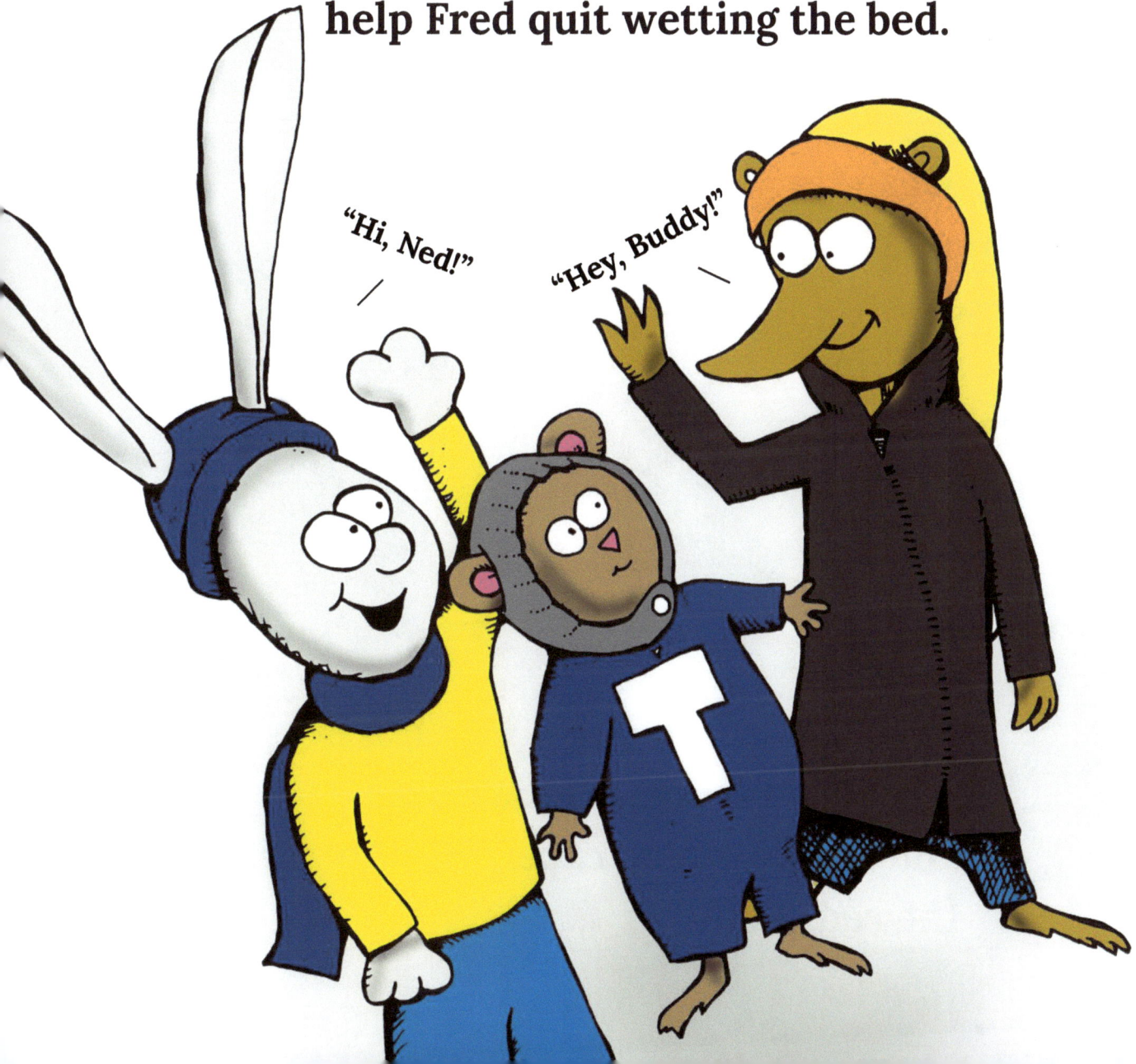

"Hi, Ned!"

"Hey, Buddy!"

Ned, who wasn't always nice to Fred, lived down the street behind the house with the red shed.

A crooked fence, a squeaky sled, and a bedwetting *expert* beside the red shed.

Ned told Fred that wetting the bed was all in his head... Fred thought about it for a moment and slowly said... "Well, I guess it makes sense, Ned, it must be all in my head!"

"Trust me!"

"Make's sense, I guess."

"Drink as much juice as you want before bed... I promise it will be fine!"

"Apple, grape, and lemonade... Drink it all!" young Ned had said.

Fred trusted Ned and drank
a jug of juice before bed!
The jug went empty. Every
drop! Fred's tummy felt like
it might pop!

"Clug! Clug! Clug!"

During the night, to Fred's surprise,
Ned turned out to be full of lies!

Fred rolled left.

Fred rolled right.

Something didn't feel quite right...

A river of potty started to pour
as if from a spout...

It bubbled, it splashed, it
whooshed instead...

"OH NO!" yelled poor sleepy
Fred.

Potty covered the sheets...

What's that **all about?**

The blanket floated like a boat, Fred
thought he may need a raincoat!

Tinkle sprinkled
all over the place!

"It's happening, again!"

Fred jumped to his feet, to the toilet he raced. He zigged past toys, he zagged past a chair, while potty drops flew everywhere!

Potty flew down the hall, hitting the ceiling, splashing the wall. It even hit the light. What a wild and soggy night!

"Why does this keep happening?"

Fred cried.

"I try and try!"
poor Fred had
said. "But still, my
bladder throws a
party in my bed!"

The next day, Fred sped down the street to talk to Ned and along the way, he met Ted.

His scooter went thump, his heart went dread... He was going to have a word with that tricky Ned!

When Fred saw the house with the
red shed, he spotted Ned standing
on the hill getting ready to sled.

"Later, dudes!"

Escaping quickly, Ned flew away on his sled going so fast his hat held on by a thread! His sled went zoom, his scarf went shred. Snow flew up around mean Ned.

"Ha Ha!" laughed Ned
with a bouncing head.
"Better luck tomorrow,
bed-wetting Fred!"

Ned laughed all the
way down the hill
while riding his sled.
He made fun of Fred
for wetting the bed.

Fred hung his head and said goodbye to Ted! He sniffled loud, his eyes turned red, "I wish I had a dryer bed."

"I'm so sorry!"

"I'm going home!"

Dad walked in with a grin... he told Fred to hold up his chin.

He held the jug above his head, "Mystery solved!" his father said.

Dad held the empty jug of juice. He told Fred that too much juice makes potty come loose like a runaway fire hose caboose!

Dad gave Fred some good advice and just to make sure he told Fred twice...

1. You are not alone! Don't worry, it will get better.
2. Everyone has wet the bed! It's normal. Yes, even Ned has wet the bed.
3. Drink less before bedtime.
4. Potty right before you go to bed.
5. If you feel the need to potty in the night, get up and go potty.
6. Don't fret if you have an accident, you can try again tomorrow.
7. Never let wetting the bed steal your joy in life.
8. Your body is still learning, and learning takes time.

"I love you!"

I wish we could say that Fred never wet the bed again, but that wouldn't be true. Accidents still happened, but Fred no longer felt blue.

If you are like Fred and struggle with wetting the bed, then this book is just for you. Even the person telling this story once had the same problem, too!

DRY NIGHT TRACKER

Let's see how many *dry nights* you can have!

S	M	T	W	T	F	S
☆	☆	☆	☆	☆	☆	☆
☆	☆	☆	☆	☆	☆	☆
☆	☆	☆	☆	☆	☆	☆
☆	☆	☆	☆	☆	☆	☆

Great Job! 🏆 Reward: _____

Read more books from Craig Biss...

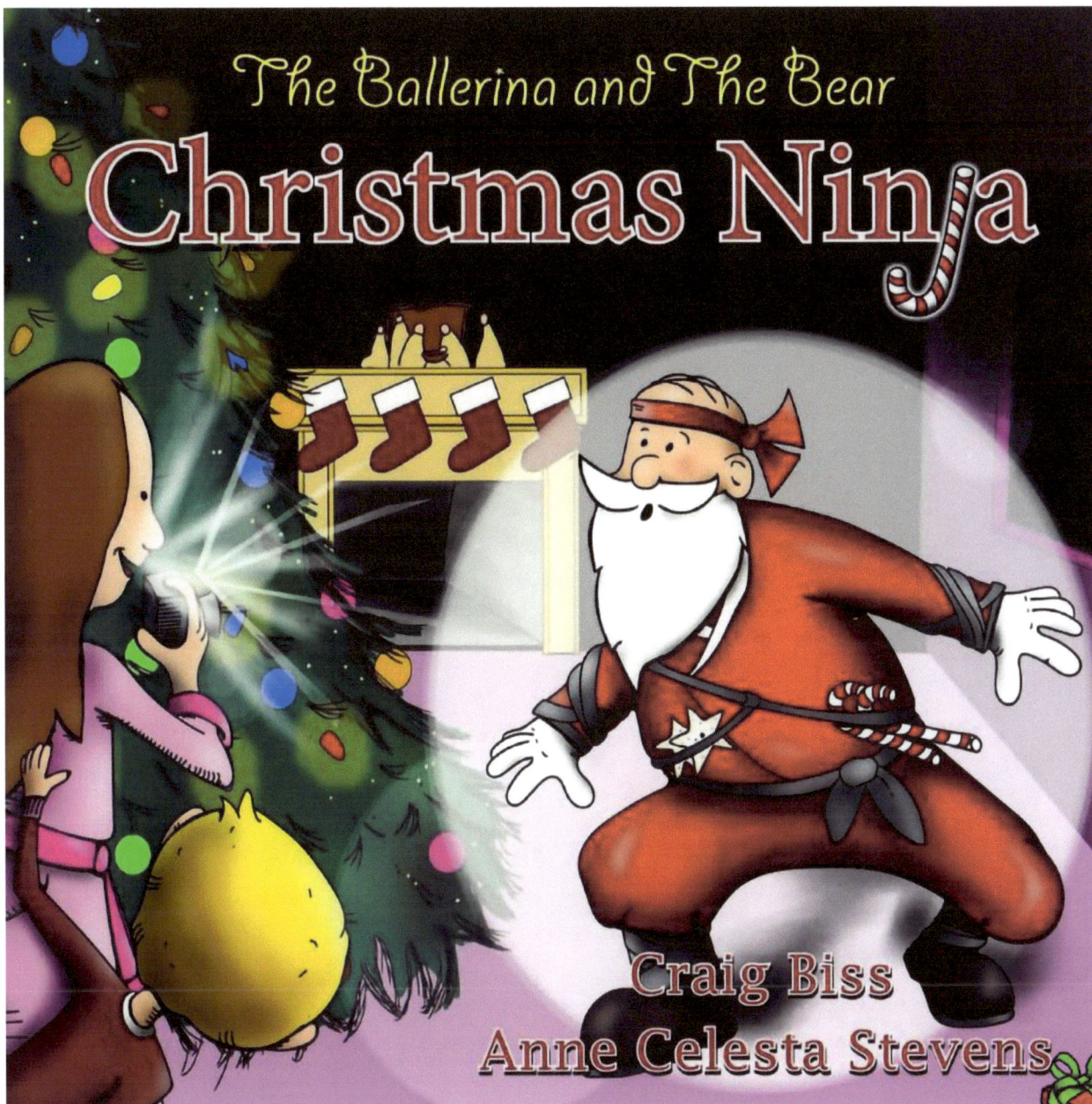

The Ballerina and The Bear
Christmas Ninja

Craig Biss
Anne Celesta Stevens

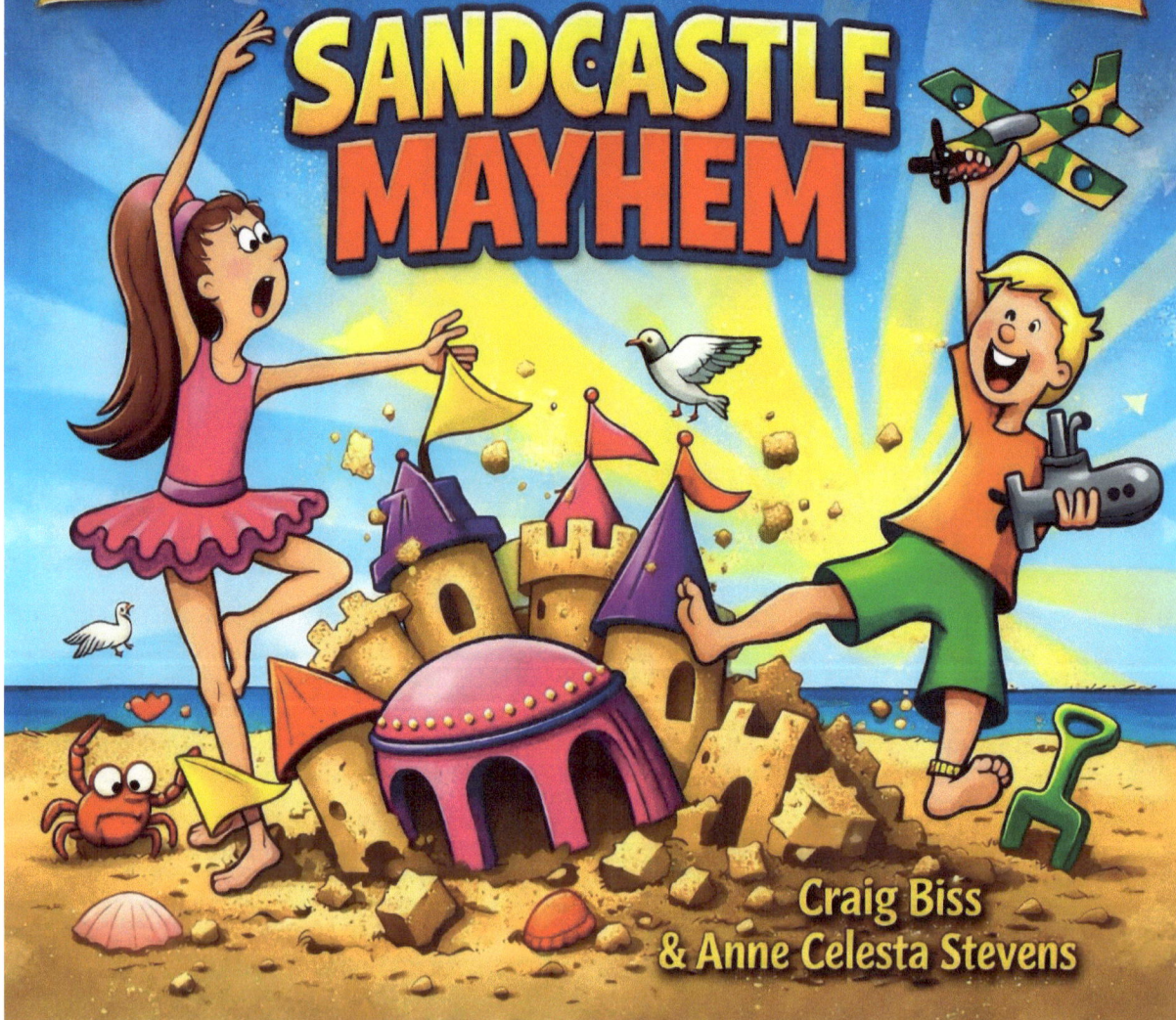

This book ends here. If you choose to leave an honest review on Amazon, thank you!

www.ingramcontent.com/pod-product-compliance
Lightning Source LLC
Chambersburg PA
CBHW041551040426
42447CB00002B/132

9781949439052